MILITARY ENGINEERING IN ACTION
★ ★ ★

CYBER TECHNOLOGY

USING COMPUTERS TO FIGHT TERRORISM

Judy Silverstein Gray and Taylor Baldwin Kiland

Enslow Publishing
101 W. 23rd Street
Suite 240
New York, NY 10011
USA

enslow.com

Acknowledgements

Special thanks to Jackson Edward Kiland for his insight, wisdom, and enthusiasm—you made this book better! We'd also like to express our deepest gratitude to the venerable Rich Gray for his valued perspective and thought-provoking questions. Finally, we could not have produced this book without Zac Dannelly, who is one of the US Navy's best.

Published in 2017 by Enslow Publishing, LLC.
101 W. 23rd Street, Suite 240, New York, NY 10011

Library of Congress Cataloging-in-Publication Data

Names: Gray, Judy Silverstein, author. | Kiland, Taylor Baldwin, 1966- author.
Title: Cyber technology : using computers to fight terrorism / Judy Silverstein Gray and Taylor Baldwin Kiland.
Description: New York, NY : Enslow Publishing, 2017. | Series: Military engineering in action | Includes bibliographical references and index.
Identifiers: LCCN 2016012431| ISBN 9780766075382 (library bound) | ISBN 9780766075351 (pbk.) | ISBN 9780766075368 (6-pack)
Subjects: LCSH: Cyberspace operations (Military science)—Juvenile literature. | Cyberterrorism—Juvenile literature. | Terrorism—United States—Prevention—Juvenile literature.
Classification: LCC U163 .G75 2017 | DDC 363.325—dc23
LC record available at https://lccn.loc.gov/2016012431

Photos Credits: Cover, p. 1 Vjom/Shutterstock.com (global network), KANIN.studio/Shutterstock.com (ranger with tablet); art/background throughout Dianka Pyzhova/Shutterstock.com, Ensuper/Shutterstock.com, foxie/Shutterstock.com, kasha_malasha/Shutterstock.com, pashabop/Shutterstock.com; p. 2 Aaron Amat/Shutterstock.com; p. 5 U.S. Army photo by Mike Strasser/USMA PAO; p. 7 Marshad Huq; pp. 8, 19 GlebStock/Shutterstock.com; p. 11 WindVector/Shutterstock.com; p. 12 PhotoQuest/Getty Images; p. 14 JEWEL SAMAD/AFP/Getty Images; p. 17 Apic/Getty Images; p. 18 US Air Force/Senior Airman Brett Clashman; p. 22 DoD/Senior Airman Franklin R. Ramos, US Air Force; p. 24 BORIS ROESSLER/AFP/Getty Images; p. 25 Ken James/Bloomberg/Getty Images; pp. 28–29, 41 Chip Somodevilla/Getty Images; p. 30 Chang W. Lee/Pool/Getty Images; p. 32 DVIDS; p. 33 US Navy/Mass Communication Specialist 2nd Class David R. Finley Jr.; p. 36 US Army/Mike Strasser/USMA PAO; p. 37 Matthew J. Lee/The Boston Globe/Getty Images; p. 38 US Air Force/Naoko Shimoji.

CONTENTS

Cyber Sleuth

Imagine you have just spent a few days sharpening your technical skills at a government-sponsored "hackathon" in San Francisco, networking with other "cyberwarriors" who support military special operations. You learned new wireless protocols, fended off network attacks in a blue team exercise, and now you're ready to share what you've learned with your command. Armed with a healthy dose of confidence, you log on at work and start receiving e-mails and direct messages from people you met over the last week. One is from a gal named Denise: *"Hi. I met u last Friday at the conference and we talked about debugging my website scripts. Here's the new code we discussed. Would love ur input!!! :)"*

A West Point cadet competes during the annual Cyber Defense Exercise. The information technology, computer science, and electrical engineering majors are tasked with defending a computer network against an opposition force that consists of National Security Agency (NSA) and Department of Defense personnel.

You remember. You posted some stuff online right after that really interesting debugging lecture, and you recall Denise saying she was out of business cards but would send her contact info and some information about her most recent project. You open the attachment and do not notice any immediate errors in her script.

You forward it to a few colleagues to see if they can see the problem with Denise's code. After all, it *seemed* legitimate. An hour later, your phone rings and it's your IT department. It seems the attachment you opened was a fast-moving virus to exfiltrate important and sensitive data from the command's computers.

While this scenario is imaginary, it's also plausible, according to Navy Ensign Zac Dannelly, a 2016 Naval Academy graduate and a member of the university's first group of cyber operations majors. He trained for four years to understand and mitigate the risks of this type of attack, which used both technical and social vulnerabilities. He has worked through many scenarios like this that tested his cyber defense skills. "The more realistic the situation," he says of cyber games, "the greater you understand the need to balance your decision-making capabilities."

Ensign Dannelly is the tenth generation in his family to serve in the military—a lineage dating back to the French and Indian War in the 1700s. Like his ancestors, he is excited about serving his country and serving on the front lines. But rather than on the beaches of a foreign shore, he is fighting within the cyber frontier, having recently become an information warfare officer in the US Navy. "My generation has grown up in this domain, played in it, worked with it and has a very intimate connection to cyber," he says. Passionate and committed, he knows he's exactly where he belongs. His work uses his strong math and analytical skills, as well as an interest in human interactions, policy, the arts, and literature. "It doesn't just involve a computational aspect, it engages curiosity and a willingness to explore," says Ensign Dannelly. It has also given him a broader perspective because our entire society is connected by computers. Damage to information networks can affect a nation's economy and daily functionality. He examines previous network attacks and how problems were solved. And he's not afraid to tap into his creative streak, to close network security gaps, contain a breach, or develop a system to better analyze information.

Zac Dannelly is assigned to the navy's US Fleet Cyber Command. He is on the cutting edge of cyberwarfare issues.

Whether at a conference or at his first assignment at the navy's Tenth Fleet, the US Fleet Cyber Command, Ensign Dannelly thinks like a detective. He asks himself basic questions: who, what, and why? Who carried out the attack or intrusion, and was it a nation state, a hacktivist group, or an individual? What information was accessed, and did it affect the entire system or just a portion?

How was the data changed? Where was the source of the breach? Did it involve private computer networks, government networks, or classified data? Finally, Ensign Dannelly asks himself, "Who has jurisdiction in the case? Which agencies should be engaged in tackling the problem? Who should be held accountable for the breach?" In other words, he's preparing himself to be more than just a coder or a code breaker. He's preparing to be on the cutting edge of cyberwarfare as a leader in this growing career field.

Cyberwarriors must stay one step ahead of criminals around the world who are ready to attack the United States through the Internet.

Three Basic Elements of Cybersecurity

Our world is wired and interconnected, and people and their devices are linked together. Yet sometimes, the interconnections are exactly where threats to security occur. Computer network defense (CND) offers a strategy to deter cyberattacks and maintain confidence in the confidentiality, availability, and integrity of friendly networks such as phones, laptops, and software for users to access.

Computer network exploitation (CNE) is a form of spying because it uses a network to proactively extract and gather intelligence with significant financial, reputation, or political consequences.

A computer network attack (CNA) is similar but is designed to actually disrupt, deny, degrade, or destroy enemy networks, which could sabotage the ability to be productive or to access important information.

The implications of cybersecurity are far-reaching, extending to nearly every aspect of US security. A good system can help strengthen the country's power grid, nuclear defense, and air traffic control system. And it's evolving on a nearly daily basis. That's why cyberwarriors must be eternally vigilant, staying one step ahead of enemies lurking around the world with the ability to attack the United States with a single weapon: an Internet connection.

Decoding the Cyber Domain

Throughout history, people have always searched for ways to send secret communications in code. That's because for as long as the military has communicated, enemy spies have tried to intercept messages. Crafting ways to conceal messages is vital to ensuring the secrecy of military operations. You could say the smoke signals Native Americans used were one of the first forms of secret communications and the oldest form of long-distance communications. They were also used by the Chinese, ancient Greeks, and the Japanese and Germans during World War I.

As technology became more sophisticated, so did the means of transmitting messages. Once electricity was discovered in the nineteenth century, a new form of communication called Morse

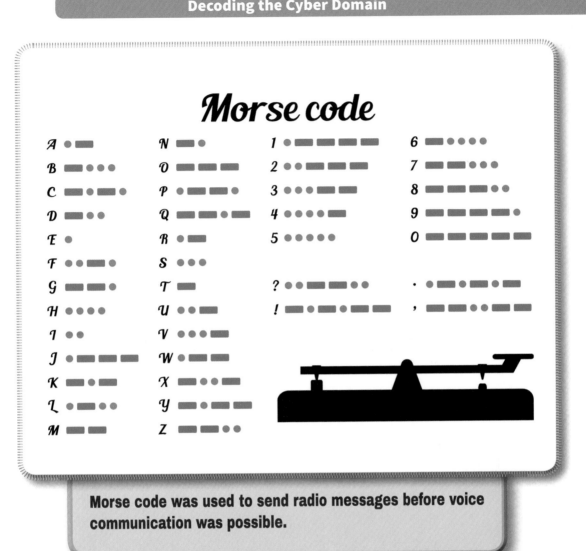

Morse code

A	●▬	N	▬●	1	●▬▬▬▬	6	▬●●●●
B	▬●●●	O	▬▬▬	2	●●▬▬▬	7	▬▬●●●
C	▬●▬●	P	●▬▬●	3	●●●▬▬	8	▬▬▬●●
D	▬●●	Q	▬▬●▬	4	●●●●▬	9	▬▬▬▬●
E	●	R	●▬●	5	●●●●●	0	▬▬▬▬▬
F	●●▬●	S	●●●				
G	▬▬●	T	▬	?	●●▬▬●●	·	●▬●▬●▬
H	●●●●	U	●●▬	!	▬●▬●▬▬	,	▬▬●●▬▬
I	●●	V	●●●▬				
J	●▬▬▬	W	●▬▬				
K	▬●▬	X	▬●●▬				
L	●▬●●	Y	▬●▬▬				
M	▬▬	Z	▬▬●●				

Morse code was used to send radio messages before voice communication was possible.

code was widely adopted. Developed by Samuel F. B. Morse, it uses a series of electric "pulses" that can be sent through a wire. The pulses are various combinations of short and long signals. The arrangements of these pulses—along with the silences in between them—translate into letters of the alphabet. This system was used extensively for transmitting messages on a radio before it was possible to communicate using voice.

Navajo Code Talkers

During World War II, radios and telephones were the most frequently used machines to transmit messages about battle plans and troop movements. It was difficult to keep these plans secret because the enemy could easily eavesdrop on the conversations. The US military needed a code that could not be broken, so they chose Navajo, a language few understood. In 1942, the military recruited four hundred Navajo Indians to serve in the Marine Corps as "code talkers." They developed and memorized an encrypted code based on the Navajo language. A short message could be encoded,

Private First Class Preston Toledo and Private First Class Frank Toledo, cousins and Navajo Indians, relay orders over a field radio in their native language in 1943.

transmitted, and decoded in twenty seconds. It was first used in the Battle of Iwo Jima in the Pacific, where hundreds of messages were sent and received—with no errors. The code was never deciphered by the Japanese, and the Navajo code talkers are credited with significantly assisting the Allied war effort. President George W. Bush awarded the code talkers the Congressional Gold Medal in 2001.

The Enigma of the Enigma

One of the most notoriously difficult code machines for the Allied coalition to break was called Enigma. Named for the word that means "a person or thing that is mysterious, puzzling, or difficult to understand," it was invented by a German engineer named Arthur Scherbius at the end of World War I. The Nazi Germany military adopted it for use during World War II. The code used to decipher the message changed every day. German operators would be given a plaintext message to encrypt. The operator would depress each letter key, which was scrambled to produce a random substitute, based upon the unique wiring of the machine. Each subsequent letter that was pressed—or entered—into the machine would advance the rotor slightly and activate a different electrical pathway. Each one of these pathways would produce a different letter substitution. Each letter represented an entirely new code. Although it looked like a series of randomly assembled letters, it was an easily transmitted message using a variety of code. The German operator who decoded messages needed an Enigma machine with the same synchronized settings so that the process could be reversed. That helped to accurately decipher the plaintext message.

The key to maintaining the secrecy of the Enigma machines was a list of daily key settings and instruction documents, which were heavily guarded by the Germans. The code and the machines were considered to be unbreakable.

Working at Britain's code-breaking center in an old mansion about 50 miles (80 kilometers) northwest of London, British

Although considered unbreakable, the code used by the German Enigma machine was cracked, and the Allied forces ultimately defeated the Nazis.

computer scientist Alan Turing and his team of engineers worked feverishly to devise techniques to break the code. It included their own electromechanical device, and it identified the daily settings on the Enigma machines. They were able to crack the code in 1941 and intercept German messages. This information helped enable Allied forces to defeat the Nazis. Some historians have said that the work accomplished by Turing and his team shortened the war by two to four years.

FACT

The Zimmerman Telegram

In early 1917, a coded telegram sent to Mexico by Arthur Zimmerman, the foreign secretary of the German Empire, was intercepted and decoded by British and American intelligence. The Zimmerman telegram appealed to the Mexican government to declare war on the United States. The goal was to distract the United States from World War I and tie up its resources, thus preventing the United States from assisting Britain and other European allies in their war against the Germans. The contents of the decrypted telegram were made public, and Americans were outraged. As a result, the United States entered World War I more quickly.

Code Breaking on the Ocean Floor

During the Cold War, spying and covert intelligence gathering by both the Soviet Union and the United States was rampant. Nuclear submarines were a critical asset used during the Cold War to track other ship movements, maintain a nuclear presence in international waters, and intercept communications by the enemy. They did this by tapping into top-secret undersea telephone cables that the Soviet Union's military laid on the floor of the Barents Sea. In the book *Blind Man's Bluff: The Untold Story of American Submarine Espionage*, authors Christopher Drew and Sherry Sontag reveal how the US Navy "bugged" these cables with secret listening devices in the 1960s, allowing them to gather vitally important information on Soviet military operations. Special warfare divers aboard submarines made daring deep-water dives to attach the listening devices to the undersea cables on the ocean floor. US naval intelligence officials were able to identify Soviet military plans. You could call it a very early form of hacking.

Worms, Viruses, and Trojan Horses

Computer hacking became a greater threat when computers became connected to each other through the vast network we now call the Internet. When created, only government employees were using the system, then called ARPANET. Initially, it was named for the government agency where it was created: DARPA (the Defense Advanced Research Project Agency). With such a small number of people using ARPANET, most of whom knew each other, there was no real perceived need or demand for security. In March of 1971, that all changed.

ARPANET users arrived at work one morning and found a mysterious message on their computer screens saying, "I'm the creeper. Catch me if you can!" It was an experiment, run by a computer engineer named Bob Thomas who wanted to test the theory that data can duplicate itself. The "Creeper" spread to ten

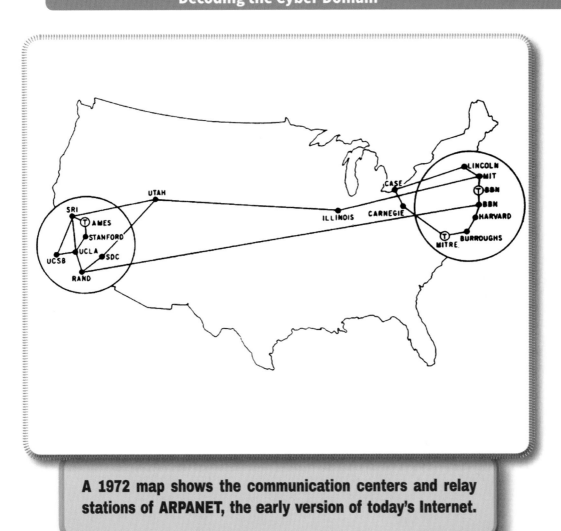

A 1972 map shows the communication centers and relay stations of ARPANET, the early version of today's Internet.

computers, causing havoc. It was called a "virus" because it spread like an illness, "infecting" the entire computer system. Although this was the first time an unidentified person placed malicious computer code onto the newly formed Internet, it was certainly not the last.

In 1988, a graduate student at Cornell University named Robert Morris Jr. wrote an experimental, self-replicating computer program and inserted it into the Internet. At the time, it was still a system used mostly by the government and universities. Morris made the program seem as if it originated at the Massachusetts Institute of Technology (MIT) to hide the real origins. Morris claimed he created the virus to see how big the Internet was. The program spread like a wildfire, replicating quickly and infecting many university, military, and medical research machines, slowing them down or crashing them. Called the Morris Worm, it was estimated to have affected two thousand computers within fifteen hours. Morris was convicted of computer fraud and abuse.

This cyber protection team is working on defense procedures at Nellis Air Force Base in Nevada. Their goal is to prevent potential space, cyberspace, and missile threats against United States and Allied forces.

What Is Hacking?

You have probably read a lot about hackers and hacking. You might have even heard someone say, "I've been hacked." But what does the term "hack" mean? By definition, hackers are people who are proficient at using or programming a computer. They use their skills to gain unauthorized access to a computer network or file. The computer industry started using the slang term "hacking" in the 1960s as a nickname for someone who is particularly skilled at computer programming. It is likely derived from the golf term "hack," which means "to chop," or from the golf term "hacker," which means "an amateur player." Later, the term "hack" came to mean someone in the computer industry who played harmless pranks or broke into computer networks for fun. Eventually, it meant someone who has more devious and illegal computer activity in mind. "Black hat" hackers use their knowledge to breach or bypass an individual's or organization's Internet security without permission. Sometimes, their efforts are coordinated with others. "White hat" hackers work on behalf of government organizations or companies to uncover vulnerabilities. These people are also called ethical hackers.

One year later, in October 1989, an antinuclear group hacked into the computers of the US Department of Energy and the National Aeronautics and Space Administration (NASA). When employees logged into their computers, they were greeted with a screen that read, "WORMS AGAINST NUCLEAR KILLERS ... Your System Has Been Officially WANKed." The group had decided to take their political protests online. This was one of the first instances of "hacktivism," or breaking into a computer for a political or socially motivated purpose.

Militaries, governments, and corporations around the world started to wake up to the fact that these individuals and rogue groups could cause real damage—to equipment and productivity. Governments recognized that hackers were not just motivated by making money. Hacktivism gave these groups notoriety and a certain degree of power and control. That's when governments, the military, and organizations realized the risk to sensitive and secret information could be a digital form of espionage.

CHAPTER 30

Network Attacks: Are You Being "Phished"?

Warfare in the twenty-first century is no longer conducted only on battlefields. Increasingly, it is waged between enemy nations in cyberspace. During the last decade, there have been a series of dangerous cyberwarfare attacks on public and private computer networks in the United States and other nations. Many have involved malware, short for "malicious software." It is hostile or intrusive, and it is typically embedded in harmless or useful software that attaches itself to the user's computer. Hackers use a variety of devious methods to break into a computer or network, including "phishing." In a phishing expedition, a hacker will send an e-mail that appears to come from a friend or colleague with a

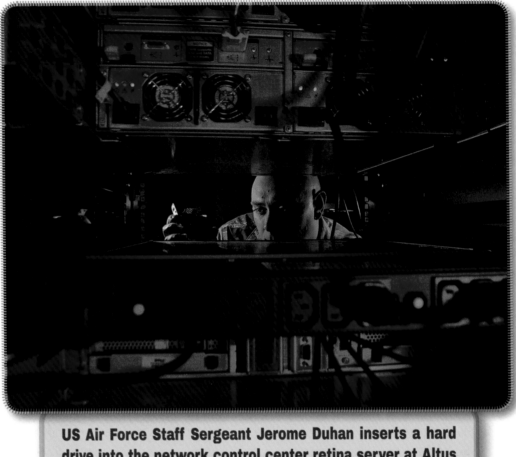

US Air Force Staff Sergeant Jerome Duhan inserts a hard drive into the network control center retina server at Altus Air Force Base, Oklahoma. He is preparing for a command cyber readiness inspection.

request to open an attachment or click on a link. Once the recipient opens or clicks, malware invades the computer and tracks the user's behavior on the computer, extracts private information, or shuts down the computer completely. It can even force the computer to perform tasks without the user's knowledge. This is how "botnets" are formed.

Botnets are a collection of many computers infected with malware that follow the demands of a malicious third party. Some botnets have infected more than five hundred thousand computers, all controlled by one person. Botnets can be used to spy on people, spam computers, steal private or confidential information, or shut down computers. These armies of hijacked computers can attack even more computers and networks, creating a flood of requests to a particular network or website. Overwhelmed, the targeted network or website can crash or deny legitimate users access. This is called a distributed denial of service (DDoS) attack.

A DDoS occurred in 2007 against the tiny Baltic country of Estonia, formerly part of the Soviet Union. The attack shut down the websites of the nation's newspapers, banks, the president and parliament, and various government ministries. It was devastating because Estonia is particularly advanced in its use of computers and networks and highly dependent on the functionality of its information technology networks. The Russian government was the suspected culprit, since the two countries had been recently engaged in disputes. Full of technology-savvy specialists, the people and government of Estonia were able to recover, but the cyberattack was a wake-up call for governments and militaries around the world. Safeguarding a nation's technology networks requires military-level protection—the same type of protection a military provides its nation's geographic borders.

America and its allies around the world are not always the intended targets of cyberattacks. One of the most severe attacks on a computer network is rumored to have been initiated by the United States (and Israel). In fact, some experts say it was the first time a cyberattack was used as a "digital weapon." Though the United States government and its military will not admit to conducting attacks against the nation's enemies, there is enough evidence to suggest that the 2010 Stuxnet virus appeared to have targeted Iran's top-secret nuclear facilities and, specifically, its nuclear centrifuges.

A screen displays the activities of a botnet during a workshop on computers and cybercrimes. A botnet is a collection of infected computers that are often used to send repetitive tasks or spam e-mails.

These sophisticated cylindrical machines are used to enrich uranium, the first step in the process to produce nuclear weapons. The virus targeted the computer systems that control and monitor the speed of the centrifuges. Iran has been in stubborn pursuit of a nuclear weapons program, and the United States and its allies are eager to stop the rogue nation's progress. The Stuxnet virus effectively shut down the centrifuges. It was the first time malware caused significant physical damage to a facility.

Is It a Computer Virus or a Worm?

While "virus" and "worm" are frequently used interchangeably to describe a computer program that infects and disables a computer, there are some subtle differences. Both are maliciously created by people who want to disrupt business, military, and government operations. A virus attaches itself to an executable file, requiring a human to open and run it. It travels from one computer to another, leaving infections along the way.

A worm is considered a subclass of a virus, but the difference is it doesn't require human action to spread. It can travel from one computer to another without human assistance because it takes advantage of information transportation systems located on the computer system. It is particularly dangerous because it can replicate itself hundreds or thousands of times, filling up a large amount of computer memory.

Computer repairs can be required after a system is infected with a virus.

In June 2015, the US Office of Personnel Management (OPM), the government agency that hires government employees and manages their security clearances, announced that hackers had broken into its computers, compromising more than twenty-one million records. Stolen information included Social Security numbers, addresses, and fingerprints. It was the largest breach of government information ever, and its effects are still being felt. Investigators suspect the Chinese government of perpetrating the attack.

Fighting Cyberterrorism and Defending the Nation's Networks

Cybersecurity experts worry every day about the threat to the United States' computer networks. Just as it is almost impossible to track every terrorist around the world who might try to injure or kill Americans, it is almost impossible to track every potential hacker and enemy nation who wants to harm the country. The country's power grid, nuclear power plants, water systems, transportation systems, online commerce systems, stock market, and cell phone networks are all at risk because they depend on computer networks to run. It's going to take an "army" of highly trained and highly vigilant cyberwarriors to protect the nation.

A display of the seals of the US Cyber Command, the National Security Agency, and the Central Security Service stands in front of the government buildings in Maryland.

But the war on terrorism in cyberspace requires both offensive and defensive capabilities. While the defense of the nation's networks remains important, we must also use the most current technology to hunt for terrorists both within the United States and abroad. Monitoring their activities in cyberspace is vital to defense.

Searching for terrorists throughout cyberspace is conducted by collecting information about them. But this is only effective if adversaries don't know they are being watched and listened to. Otherwise, they will change their methods of communicating.

The government's primary agency for the collection of this information is the National Security Agency (NSA). The eavesdropping conducted under the NSA's international surveillance authority results in the collection of tens of millions of telephone records daily, perhaps more, to track the location of mobile devices around the world.

This bulk collection includes records of major telecommunications carriers based in the United States. The information provides data about the travel habits of telephone users and allows the NSA to create "target development" data. This is information that can lead to the identity of unknown associates of those targets the NSA *does* know about. Such monitoring of the communications of overseas militants suspected of terrorism includes accessing data from Internet companies based in the United States, including Facebook, Google, Yahoo!, and Skype.

Generally speaking, the NSA collects two types of information: content and metadata. Content is defined as the conversations that take place on telephone calls, e-mail, and online chats. It also includes online browsing histories and other search activities. Metadata describes the amassed collection of information that the NSA defines as "information about content but not the content itself." An e-mail would generate metadata information about the identities of the sender and receiver and the physical location of the sender. Similarly, telephone metadata would include the phone numbers of both the caller and receiver, as well as the length of the call. Often, the data would include the types of devices used for the conversation.

Metadata information becomes part of a vast database of devices and their locations, which allows the NSA to determine the habits of a cell phone user, as well as the phone numbers used on a regular basis. This helps the government uncover terrorist networks and allows them to track their activities.

According to an article in the *Washington Post* in 2014, the NSA has the capability to monitor and record 100 percent of a foreign

Security personnel, including the US National Guard, participate in preparations at a security operations center in New York. They were getting ready for Pope Francis's 2015 visit to the United States.

country's telephone calls, stowing thirty days' worth of calls at a time. It can also replay voices from any individual call without identifying the caller. It is important to understand the difference between "data logging" and "data mining." All the calls' metadata is "logged" for a period of time, but these telephone calls may never be listened to unless the caller starts exhibiting suspicious behavior. If he is making multiple calls to a suspected terrorist or searching on the Internet for bomb-making recipes, the NSA might actually "mine" the phone records for more clues about the caller's background, behavior, and intent. It is estimated that the NSA analysts actually listen to less than 1 percent of these recorded calls, but even that number is a lot. The NSA cuts millions of voice clips from these calls and stores them for further analysis, allowing it to build files on potential terrorists and their networks of affiliates.

On a daily basis, cyberwarriors in the military and at the NSA work in a security operations center (SOC), a type of facility where all their organization's information systems—websites, databases, networks, servers, desktops, and data centers—are monitored and defended. Those who work in analytical roles might spend their days poring over mass amounts of metadata, looking for patterns and trends to reveal the locations, behavior, and intents of known and potential terrorists.

The Navy's Top Cyberwarrior

Navy Vice Admiral Jan Tighe serves as commander of the US Navy's Fleet Cyber Command and its Tenth Fleet, the first woman to serve at the helm. Trained as a cryptologist (code breaker) at the US Naval Academy at Annapolis, she also has a PhD in electrical engineering and a master's degree in applied mathematics. She has spent most of her career defending and protecting the security of information by identifying and reducing threats, developing and promoting creative solutions to cybersecurity risks, and ensuring that cyber staff are seen as warriors on the front lines.

The National Security Agency

Established in 1952, the National Security Agency (NSA) specializes in "signals intelligence," or SIGINT. This is intelligence-gathering by the interception of signals—either communications between two people or electronic signals. The NSA monitors, collects, and processes all kinds of data for counterterrorism purposes. Some of its tactics are "passive," meaning it just listens to electronic communications. But it also maintains a physical presence all over the world where its Special Collections Service can insert eavesdropping devices in remote places.

Allegedly, this secret group engages in more aggressive tactics such as close-in surveillance, burglary, and wiretapping. In addition, it is also tasked with protecting the integrity of US government communications and information technology systems. In other words, it prevents the hacking of US networks. It is a highly secretive organization; indeed, the government did not even acknowledge its existence for many years, and employees jokingly referred to it as the "No Such Agency." It operates as part of the Department of Defense, and the director of the NSA is also the commander of the military's US Cyber Command (USCYBERCOM).

U.S. FLEET CYBER COMMAND
U.S. TENTH FLEET

Vice Admiral Jan Tighe heads the US Fleet Cyber Command. Tighe is the first female commander of a numbered fleet in US Navy history.

Vice Admiral Tighe states that adaptability and the ability to solve puzzles, think critically, and visualize behavior patterns are critical to becoming a successful cyberwarrior. Vice Admiral Tighe, along with other military cyberwarriors, recognizes that cyberspace is now a critical warfare domain. She's grateful for serving in "such a fascinating and important field and our navy and our country have a storied history of codebreaking in defense of the nation."

Edward Snowden: Whistleblower or Traitor?

The US government employs many cyberwarriors who are entrusted to keep the nation's secrets—both the information about adversaries and collection methods. The temptation to understand secret collections of information led to a well-known case of hacking by government employees. Edward Snowden became famous—or infamous—in 2013. Was he a whistle-blower, traitor, or hero?

Opinions vary, but the facts are these: A low-level contractor working as a systems administrator for the NSA, Snowden had access to top-secret programs, information he leaked to the media. He claims he was concerned about the government's collection methods and how it invaded the average person's privacy. In response, a White House spokesman defended the bulk collection of data as an important tool to protect the country from terrorist attacks. President Obama said, "Our nation's defense depends in part on the fidelity of those entrusted with our nation's secrets. If any individual who objects to government policy can take it in their own hands to publicly disclose classified information, then we will not be able to keep our people safe, or conduct foreign policy."

Cyber Careers

As the cyber threat to the United States becomes more wide-spread and attacks become increasingly more sophisticated, the government and private companies are eager to hire skilled information technology and cybersecurity talent. There is a huge demand for cybersecurity specialists. Do you have what it takes to be a cyberwarrior?

It takes more than good video-gaming skills. Ensign Dannelly recommends: "To become a digital native, you have to speak the language, so learn some coding! No better way to grasp this domain than to understand how it is built." Furthermore, while "computer programming is fun, it gets more exciting in person. Join a robotics club!" Once you have a good foundation in coding, Dannelly believes that the discipline of tackling one computing project each month will build your cyber skills and make you competitive. Finally, he

Hands-on computer experience, along with critical thinking and problem-solving skills, are necessary for high cyber aptitude.

recommends that you harness the power of Google, a vast ocean of information to research and learn anything you want—all free and accessible to you.

In addition to hands-on computer experience, those being hired by the military and other government agencies such as the FBI and

Hackathons, Games, and Cyber Challenges

There are many ways students can test their cyber skills: hackathons, cyber camps, and cyber challenges. Also called a hack day, a hackfest, or a codefest, a hackathon is an event where computer programmers collaborate on software projects—often lasting between a day and a week. Sometimes they are held as educational forums, and sometimes they are held with the purpose of creating usable software. HackingEDU, held annually in San Mateo, California, is the world's largest educational hackathon. Major League Hacking is the official student hackathon league, providing support and mentorship to more than seventy collegiate hackathons every year.

An MIT student works on a cat bot during the annual hackathon at the MIT Student Center. The cat robot is controlled by an EKG sensor connected to the user's forearm that reads the arm motions and controls the robot.

NATIONAL CYBER SECURITY AWARENESS MONTH

AGAINST CYBER THREATS

NATIONAL CYBER SECURITY AWARENESS MONTH

PROTECT ALL INFORMATION AGAINST ATTA

PROTECT ALL INFORMATION AGAINST ATT

The goal of National Cyber Security Awareness Month, which takes place every year in October, is to spread awareness about hackers and their techniques. The goal is to reduce the number of victims in future years. There are an average of one million victims of cybercrimes in the world every day. Most of them could have prevented the attack if they were more educated on cybersecurity.

the NSA demonstrate problem-solving skills, pattern recognition, space perception, and critical thinking. The military is considering a test that would assess candidates for cyber aptitude. Recruiters are looking for candidates who not only understand how to program computer coding, but also know how to independently, patiently, and persistently troubleshoot a computer problem. Like a good detective, cyber specialists identify and follow clues to find threats and perpetrators. They love to break open computers and electronic devices, see how they work, and then reassemble them into working devices. If this description sounds like you, then a career in cybersecurity might be in your future.

Those who want to be a cybersecurity expert for the military must also demonstrate a loyalty to the nation and willingness to defend it against all enemies—foreign and domestic. Many in the military recognize the cyber battlefield will force countries to maintain vigilance against threats, while also developing a technological advantage. Cybersecurity demands staying one technical step ahead of adversaries and anticipating how and where they might attack next.

Educating the next generation of cybersecurity experts is a high priority for military leaders. The NSA offers educational programs for students to promote math, science, and language education at the elementary, middle, and high school levels. The NSA and the Department of Homeland Security (DHS) jointly sponsor the National Centers of Academic Excellence in Cyber Defense and Cyber Operations programs. Several dozen universities around the country offer these NSA- and DHS-accredited degree programs.

The Future: A Cyber Pearl Harbor?

In an October 2015 interview with the *Wall Street Journal*, Admiral Michael Rogers, commander of USCYBERCOM and director of the NSA, talked about what worries him most about today's hackers: "At the moment they seem to be focused on reconnaissance, but it's only a matter of time until someone actually does something destructive."

As the nation's top cybersecurity leader, it is his responsibility to maintain warfighting capabilities in cyberspace. He worries about enemy nations, like North Korea, Syria, and Iran, who are focused on harming the United States and its infrastructure—the electrical grid, dams, nuclear reactors, and communications networks. He thinks rogue groups such as black hat hackers, criminals, or terrorists might manipulate data on US networks, so online information may not be trusted.

Admiral Michael Rogers speaks at the Cybersecurity Technology Summit in Washington, DC.

"Non-state actors," like the Islamic State of Iraq and Syria (ISIS, also called ISIL), who want to use the Internet as a weapons system, make him take notice. Is the United States vulnerable to a "cyber Pearl Harbor" or a "digital 9/11"? Could a cyberattack as monumental and destructive to life and property and infrastructure actually happen?

The US Cyber Command

In response to a growing need to coordinate all of the government's work in cyberspace, the US military established a US Cyber Command (USCYBERCOM) in 2009. This organization's mission is to "plan, coordinate, integrate, synchronize, and conduct activities to direct the operations and defense of specified Department of Defense information networks and prepare to, and when directed, conduct full spectrum military cyberspace operations in order to enable actions in all domains, ensure US/Allied freedom of action in cyberspace and deny the same to our adversaries." Because its work crosses so many boundaries, the US Army, Navy, Air Force, and Marine Corps all have components reporting to the USCYBERCOM.

Admiral Rogers and other cybersecurity experts believe it is possible. They think we must have our "cyber weapons" ready to strike back. The work force required to support this mission is growing exponentially. The United States must have cyber experts in government and the private sector that are technically adept, agile, and creative. They must be good coders and good problem solvers, and both diligent and vigilant. As technology rapidly evolves, the need for skilled employees will grow. The cyber environment is unpredictable and rapidly changing. Having a well-trained cyber force is how the country will stay ahead of evolving risks. Training young cyberwarriors to anticipate threats, decrease vulnerabilities, and remain adaptable is the best defense.

TIMELINE

1836—Samuel Morse develops a telegraph code for communications based on electric pulses.

1941—British engineer Alan Turing breaks the German Enigma machine's code.

1942—Navajo Indians are recruited by the US military to develop a secret code based on their native language.

1952—The National Security Agency is established.

1960s—US attaches "bugs" to Soviet undersea cables, secretly collecting information on their military operations.

1971—The Creeper virus infects ten computers at the Defense Advanced Research Project Agency (DARPA).

1988—The Morris worm affects two thousand computers within fifteen hours.

1989—An antinuclear group infects Department of Energy and NASA computers in protest. It is one of the first instances of "hacktivism."

2007—The country of Estonia's government networks are anonymously attacked, shutting down the websites of its president, parliament, newspapers, banks, and various government ministries.

2009—US military establishes the US Cyber Command (USCYBERCOM).

2010—The Stuxnet virus shuts down Iranian nuclear centrifuges.

2013—The Anonymous group hacks Target Corporation, stealing more than forty million customer credit card numbers.

2014—Hard drives on computers at Sony Pictures are crippled by a cyberattack, where personal information and e-mails are stolen and released to the public.

2015—Computers at the US Office of Personnel Management (OPM) are hacked, compromising more than twenty-one million records.

botnet—A very large group of interconnected and centrally controlled computers enlisted to carry out large-scale tasks of a repetitive nature.

cyberattack—A hostile act using a computer to disrupt, disable, or destroy another computer or network.

cybersecurity—Actions taken to provide safety and security for information and the network where it is stored.

cyberterrorism—According to the FBI definition, it is the "premeditated, politically motivated attack against information, computer systems, computer programs, and data which results in violence against non-combatant targets by sub-national groups or clandestine agents."

distributed denial of service (DDoS) attack—An attempt to make a computer or network unavailable to its intended user by sending it an unmanageable amount of false traffic. Usually carried out by a botnet.

hacker—Someone who is proficient at using or programming a computer and uses these skills to gain unauthorized access to a computer network or file.

hacktivism—The practice of breaking into a computer for political reasons or social purposes.

Internet—The global communication network that allows almost all computers around the world to connect with one another and share information. The first such network was started in the 1960s by a US government agency called DARPA.

malware—Short for malicious software, this is hostile or intrusive software typically embedded in harmless or useful software that attaches itself to the user's computer. It can track a user's behavior on a computer, steal private information, or shut down the computer.

metadata—Data that provides information about other data; the word was first used in 1983.

phishing—Using e-mail to trick a computer user into disclosing personal information by pretending to come from a trusted source. It may look legitimate based upon its design or wording.

FURTHER READING

BOOKS

Kaplan, Fred. *Dark Territory: The Secret History of Cyber War*. New York, NY: Simon & Schuster, 2016.

Singer, P. W., and Allan Friedman. *Cybersecurity and Cyberwar: What Everyone Needs to Know*. Bethesda, MD: Oxford University Press, 2014.

Zetter, Kim. *Countdown to Zero Day: Stuxnet and the Launch of the World's First Digital Weapon*. New York, NY: Broadway Books, 2015.

WEBSITES

Department of Homeland Security
dhs.gov/stopthinkconnect
This website educates Americans about how to be safe online.

National Security Agency
www.nsa.gov/academia/early_opportunities/index.shtml
The NSA offers K–12 educational programs for kids interested in careers in cybersecurity.

Sites for Kids to Learn How to Code
code.org
codecademy.com
instructables.com/tag/type-id/category-technology
These websites offer kids the fun and interactive opportunity to learn how to code.

INDEX